# GOD IN THE WAR:

PREACHED IN BEHALF OF

## THE U. S. CHRISTIAN COMMISSION

ON THE DAY OF

## THE NATIONAL THANKSGIVING,

August 6th, 1863,

BY REV. HENRY SMITH, D. D.

Pastor of the North Presbyterian Church,

BUFFALO, N. Y.

*PUBLISHED BY REQUEST.*

BUFFALO:
PRINTING HOUSE OF WHEELER, MATTHEWS & WARREN,
*Office of the Commercial Advertiser.*
1863.

# Correspondence.

BUFFALO, August 7th, 1863.

HENRY SMITH, D. D.:

DEAR SIR: The undersigned, having listened with great pleasure to your sermon on the day of National Thanksgiving, and believing that the cause of Freedom, Truth and Christian Patriotism demand that it be placed in a form for general circulation, respectfully ask that you will furnish a copy for the press.

| | | | |
|---|---|---|---|
| G. W. HEACOCK, | PASCAL P. PRATT, | D. D. LORE, | S. H. FISH, |
| CLARK KENDALL, | EDWARD P. BEALS, | ARTHUR BURTIS, | B. TIMMERMAN, |
| HUGH WEBSTER, | HENRY H. MARTIN, | S. G. AUSTIN, | ZENAS CLARK, |
| J. F. PETER, | AARON RUMSEY, | JASON SEXTON, | H. STILLMAN, |
| JOHN G. DESHLER, | MOSES BRISTOL, | C. E. YOUNG, | JESSE KETCHUM. |
| JAS. D. SAWYER, | THOMAS FARNHAM, | A. D. A. MILLER, | |

BUFFALO, August 7th, 1863.

MESSRS. D. D. LORE, G. W. HEACOCK, AND OTHERS:

GENTLEMEN: Thanking you for your kind judgment of my Thanksgiving Discourse, and earnestly praying that it may contribute something toward the "cause of Freedom, Truth and Christian Patriotism," I place the manuscript at your disposal.

HENRY SMITH.

# DISCOURSE.

The Lord shall cause thine enemies that rise up against thee to be smitten before thy face: they shall come out against thee one way, and flee before thee seven ways. DEUT. XXVIII. 7.

THE proclamation of the President of the United States, in obedience to whose recommendation we are assembled to-day, has been read in your hearing. It is a noble, Christian document, fully recognizing our national dependence upon God, and clearly asserting a solemn conviction, on the part of our rulers, that a divine and Almighty power, instinct with the attributes of ever-living justice and ever-living mercy, presides over the destinies of nations. I ask you carefully to note its doctrines. It maintains that this divine Power is an ever-active Power, interposing continually in the affairs of men; for it ascribes our victories to his hand, outstretched in answer to the prayers of his people. "It has pleased Almighty God to hearken to the supplications and prayers of an afflicted people, and to vouchsafe to the army and navy of the United States victories on the land and on the sea, so signal and so effective as to furnish reasonable grounds for augmented confidence that the Union of these States will be maintained, their Constitution preserved, and their peace and prosperity permanently secured." It maintains that this Power is a just Power, which, in the grievous afflictions we have suffered, has only visited upon us a meet retribution for our national sins; for it counsels us to ask of Him to-day, "to lead the whole nation through paths of repentance and submission to the Divine will, back to the perfect enjoyment of union and fraternal peace." It affirms that this Power is a wise one; for it solicits our petitions at the throne of God, that He will "guide the counsels of the Government with wisdom adequate to so great a national emergency." It maintains that this is a merciful Power; for it asks us to implore Him, "to visit with tender care and consolation, throughout the length and breadth of our land, all those who, through the vicissitudes of marches, voyages, battles and sieges, have been brought to suffer in mind, body or estate."

My friends, is this all a dream of our rulers? Is it only an irrepressible outburst of human feeling, conscious of deliverance, and yet conscious of its own impotence to command success? rejoicing over victories achieved, and yet fully aware that when the scale of battle hung vibrating between success and disaster, the weight of a feather would have carried the equilibrium against us, ascribes the make-weight which carried it in our favor to the interposition of a power, which it knows assuredly did not lie in itself? And is this all a dream? I shall not answer the question, for I am addressing a Christian audience, who believe in God.

Is this a stroke of policy in our rulers? Having no faith in God themselves, but, as shrewd politicians, recognizing the prodigious power over the minds of the unenlightened subjects of the Government of that superstitious sentiment which men call religion, do they wish to enlist this power in favor of the cause in which they embarked? No doubt this is a possible solution of the motive of the proclamation which has summoned us to-day from the pursuits of business to the house of God. But who are our rulers? They are fellow citizens; trained in the same schools; educated under the same influences; worshipers in the same churches as ourselves. Elevated by the popular voice for a brief period to the conduct of our national affairs, they are soon again to descend to the level of subjects, and as such to reap in private life the harvest which they have sown in their public capacity: no more enlightened, no more wise, and, let us charitably hope, no less religious than ourselves.

Is this proclamation, then, the expression of a blind fanaticism, shared in alike by rulers and people, who imagine that the favor of that Almighty Power, who decides the fate of battles and controls the destiny of nations, will be propitiated by the people who make the longest prayers, and who sing the loudest *Te Deums?* and that, irrespective of the essential merits of the cause in which they are engaged? Undoubtedly this, too, is a possible supposition, for we are told that the insurgents in arms, aiming their deadly blows at the heart of their country, are no less diligent than ourselves in invoking the interposition of the Almighty; that their days of fasting at least outnumber our own. May there not be some danger, after all, since they pray so earnestly, that God will hear them; and may not their fervent, nay, frantic, petitions be accepted as proof of their sincerity? Of their sincerity, Yes. Of their acceptance with God, No. My friends, let us understand ourselves. Let us come to God to-day under no fanatical impulse. God is GOD. He is such a God as is recognized in this proclamation: a God of infinite justice, a God of infinite mercy, but a God of infinite wisdom as well. And he is a God, who, whilst forever interposing in the affairs of men, interposes in favor of, and in harmony with, the principles of divine and eternal Justice, Mercy and Wisdom. The reply of the blind man, whose eyes Christ had opened, to the Jews, is confirmed by the whole history of the world, rightly read and comprehended, as touching the divine interposition in answer to prayer: "Now we know that God heareth not sinners: but if any man be a worshiper of God, and doeth His will, him he heareth." The effectual, fervent prayer of the righteous man availeth much. That is the teaching of God's word, and that is the teaching of history. The prayer of such a man always finds an answer; not always, indeed, in the letter, but never failing in the spirit. The heart of such a man putting itself in harmony with the great principles of justice and mercy which underlie and surround and arm the government of the universe, is conscious nevertheless of a lack of wisdom, and always defers the letter of his petition to the infinite wisdom of God: saying, as touching the letter, "Not my will, but thine be done." "I never prayed more earnestly," said a true-hearted minister of Christ, in a neighboring city, "than I prayed that Sumter, with its little band of heroes under Anderson, might be preserved; and I never thanked God more earnestly than I do to-day that it fell." The foolishness of God is wiser than men, no less truly, than the weakness of God is stronger than men. Justice, Mercy, Wisdom, these are the principles in favor of which God interposes in human affairs. The voice of all history proclaims it. He who knows how to discern God's hand in history will always find it there. He who has depth enough to penetrate beneath the ripples, eddies and counter-currents which agitate the surface of affairs, and to reach the deep under-current of the great stream of human history, will feel its strong and steady flow in the direction of Justice and Mercy. He will find in that flow Human Progress. He will find in this progress a strong and steady tendency toward the realization of those two distinct momenta of human well-being, in which its great philosopher and historian finds the definition of civilization, the elevation of society, and the elevation of individual man. Before this steady flow all the obstacles which human pride, and selfishness, and wickedness, and power, have succeeded in throwing up, have been as nothing. They have been swept away by the hand of that Omnipotence which has fixed the point of its destination, or circumvented by the skill of that infinite wisdom, which has mapped out its channel. He who stands upon the deck of a steamer floating downward upon the bosom of the Father of Waters, will find its compass veering from east to west and from north to south. He who ascends to a point in the atmosphere, where its whole valley lies spread out before him, will find its broad stream marching steadily forward to the Gulf. The termination of the stream of human history has been fixed by God. Its goal is the universal, social and individual well-being of the race. Flowing through a territory upheaved and rent and channeled by human depravity, its course is guided by wisdom, which seeth not as man seeth, but by wisdom still. It is to overcome these obstacles that God interposes, and his solemn voice, uttered both in history and in his word of revealed truth, teaches us that he interposes always and only in favor of the principles of Eternal Justice and Eternal Mercy. My brethren, we have met to thank God for past successes. Do those successes lie in the line of Justice and of Mercy? If so, let us be assured that our thank-offering will be accepted. We have met to pray for further and still more signal successes. Are the successes which we desire a development of the great principles of Justice and Mercy? If so, putting ourselves under the guidance of divine wisdom, we may be assured of the final realization of our desires. We are each one of us called to act a part in human history; to contribute the mite of our individual influence to hasten or stay the progress of that great current of events, whose destination is as certain as the throne of God is stable. Have we had God's guidance in the past, so that our influence has been right? Do we desire God's guidance in the future, so that our action shall contribute to the real and permanent success for which we pray? Then are we to put ourselves in sympathy with

God. We are to lift ourselves above the shifting, and temporary, and fallible opinions of men, and understand that no prayer can be acceptable and real which does not desire the establishment of the great principles of justice and mercy; and that no success will be permanently accorded by God, which does not tend to vindicate them. In the text which has been read God promises his people success: "The Lord shall cause thine enemies that rise up against thee to be smitten before thy face: they shall come out against thee one way, and flee before thee seven ways." But is this promise without condition? Listen. "And it shall come to pass, if thou shalt hearken diligently unto the voice of the Lord thy God, to observe and to do all his commandments, which I command thee this day; that the Lord thy God will set thee on high above all the nations of the earth." The subject to which this text in its connections summons for a little time our attention is:

"THE RELIGIOUS CONDITIONS OF THE FURTHER SUCCESS OF OUR NATIONAL CAUSE."

In discussing it let us follow the analysis which has been made of the doctrines of the President's proclamation. That proclamation distinctly recognizes four great elements in the divine government of the world, as standing in a distinct and, to a Christian eye, perceptable relation to our success: God's Providence, God's Justice, God's Wisdom, and God's Mercy. Let us look a moment at each of them as a condition of our national success.

I.—*We are distinctly and truly to recognize God's Providence in this War.*

By this I mean we are distinctly and sincerely to recognize the fact of the divine interposition in determining the beginning, course, and the issue of the great struggle in which we are now engaged. We are Christians. We admit this in theory. Do we admit it in fact? Do we take it into account, not only as a real, but as omnipotent force acting continually for or against us? "Providence," said Napoleon, "is on the side of the strongest batteries." Batteries are powerful. Austerlitz, and Wagram, and Jena attest it. But what say Leipsic and Beresina? Batteries are powerful; but what did they avail him when Moscow went up to heaven in a flash of fire, and he fled to the West leaving his discomfited legions, smitten by the frown of the Almighty, to perish with frost and hunger upon the plains of Russia? Batteries are powerful, and Napoleon was a man of Destiny. He believed alike in both. On the night of the 17th of June, 1815, as from the hills of Rossomme he gazed through the darkness upon the long line of the English watch-fires, as if his spirit were riding upon the tempest, whose torrents were falling, whose lightnings were blazing, and whose thunders were pealing around him, he was heard to exclaim, "We are in sympathy, the Spirit of the Storm and I." Were they then in sympathy? That tempest proved his ruin. The fate of Waterloo hinged upon it. Well has the powerful writer who has painted the most vivid picture yet drawn of that great battle which reconstructed the map of Europe, and, as he has strongly expressed it, caused the "universe to change front," well has he said, "A few drops of water more or less prostrated Napoleon. That Waterloo should be the end of Austerlitz, Providence needed only a little rain, and an unseasonable cloud crossing the sky sufficed for the overthrow of a world." He did not dream of the consequences. The morning of the 18th of June dawned; but the provision trains, which were to refresh his drenched and hungry troops, stuck in miry roads, had not arrived. Nevertheless he was heard to say, "We have ninety chances in a hundred." Had he then forgotten the quaint saying of Frederick the Great, that "an army, like a serpent, goes upon its belly"? No, he had not forgotten. But he had faith in Destiny, and he had faith in batteries. Had he not two hundred and forty guns, whilst Wellington had but one hundred and fifty-nine. Was he not the most accomplished artillerist in the world? Was not his plan of the battle a masterpiece of strategic skill? Yet what availed his batteries and his strategy? His guns sunk in the mud, and could not be transported or handled. He must wait. The battle could not be opened till the sun approached the meridian. It was too late. Vain was the terrific storming of the heights of Mont St. Jean. Vain was the frightful bridge of the deep ditch of Ohain, filled with overthrown horses, and prostrate, crushed and perishing men, across which Ney hurled his furious squadrons of cavalry upon the foe. Vain was the unparalleled valor of the Imperial Guard. Vain was the "fury, the giddy vortex of souls and courage, and the hurricane of sword flashes." Vain was the destruction of seven-thirteenths of the English battalions. Vain were the sixty spiked cannon, and the six captured colors. Vain were the four slain horses of the Marshal Ney. Vain, every thing. It was too late. The cow-boy who guided Bulow guided him right. Blücher arrived on the field an hour too early for Napoleon, not a moment too early for the world. Waterloo was no longer a contest for victory, it was a rout and a massacre. The gray, sulphureous clouds which floated away over the vast field of carnage, formed themselves into the similitude of a desolate ocean, and of the wild crags and mountains of a rocky, barren islet. St. Helena loomed up in clear perspective over the smoking field of Waterloo. Napoleon vanished from history; and the world took a long breath.

Who won the field of Waterloo? Who hastened Blücher? Who delayed Grouchy? My friends, let me read to you the judgment of Hugo; I do not say of Hugo the Christian, but of Hugo the profound student of history. "It was time," says he, "that this vast man should fall. The excessive weight of this man in human destiny disturbed the equilibrium. * * These plethoras of all human vitality concentrated in a single head, the world mounting to the brain of one man, would be fatal to civilization, if they should endure. The moment had come for incorruptible, supreme Equity to look to it. Probably the principles and elements upon which regular gravitations in the moral order, as well as in the material, depend, began to murmur. Reeking blood, overcrowded cemeteries, weeping mothers, these are formidable pleaders. When the earth is suffering from a surcharge, there are mysterious moanings from the deeps, which the heavens do hear. Napoleon had been impeached before the Infinite, and his fall was decreed. He vexed God. Waterloo is not a battle: it is the change of front of the universe." "Waterloo is the hinge of the nineteenth century. The disappearance of the great man was necessary for the advent of the great century. One to whom there is no reply took it in charge. The panic of heroes is explained. In the battle of Waterloo there is more than a cloud, there is a meteor. God passed over it."

My friends, was God in Waterloo, and can any sane man imagine the possibility of his absence from Sumter, and Manassas, and Ball's Bluff, and the swamps of the Chickahominy; from Fort Jackson and Fort Henry; from Fort Donaldson and Shiloh; from Vicksburgh and Port Hudson; from Antietam and Gettysburg?

We are in the midst of the most tremendous upheaval of society which the nineteenth century has witnessed. If Waterloo was the hinge of the century, the rebellion in America is its open door. If the guns of Wellington and Blücher shattered its fastenings and left it ajar, the American monitors and iron-clads, whose thunders have been waked by this gigantic rebellion, will batter it to shivers, and leave a wide, blank space for the entrance of the purposes of Eternal Equity. Some say this war was unnecessary. Even this proclamation speaks of the rebellion not only as wicked, but as needless. That is the human view. Wicked it most assuredly is. Needless? Yes, in the eye of material political economy, not in the eye of God. Who left human ambition and human cupidity, aye, and human wisdom, to its own foolishness, in the repeal of the Missouri Compromise? Who distracted the counsels of the Peace Congress of Washington, and brought them to naught? Who sent an evil spirit of subserviency, blindness and dotage into the breast of the only man in the nation who had it in his power to relieve Sumter, and to nip the rebellion in the bud? Who turned back in a needless panic our undisciplined, over-confident troops, from the fatal ravine of Bull's Run? Who has kept back from us, once and again, the arm of English intervention and French intervention, raising up at critical junctures Italian complications, and Hungarian complications, and Polish complications, until the period of our defenceless weakness, and unmartial rawness and awkwardness in the science of war has gone by? Who at this moment is arraying the ancestral and traditional English hatred and jealousy of France against the aristocratic English hatred and jealousy of a democratic government, giving us hope that the second man of Destiny, the man of December, will be foiled in an attempt to establish a French despotism on these shores?

We are yet amidst the whirl and hurricane of the contest. The clouds of error and prejudice, of false opinions and false reports, obscure our vision and warp our judgments. It is yet too early to judge of the relation and bearing of events. It is yet too early to read distinctly their meaning. Men speak of the mistakes which have been made in the policy and in the conduct of the war; of the folly of the President's Emancipation Proclamation, of the failure of McClellan at Antietam, of the blunder of Meade at Gettysburg. God makes no mistakes. The folly of men is the wisdom of God. The Hugo of the next century will be able to explain to your children the meaning of our disasters as well as of our successes. He will be able to read to them the reason of the war, and expound the meaning of our final success in re-establishing the Union upon a broader and more enduring basis than it ever had before. I say our final success. I assume it. But I assume it upon this condition, that we acknowledge God in it. His hand was in its inception; his hand has been in its entire evolution; and his hand alone can conduct us through the fearful perils which still environ us to the successful issue which we so earnestly anticipate.

II.—*A second condition of success in this war is that we put ourselves in sympathy with the Justice of God.*

Men talk about Policy. My friends, God is a governor, and God is Just. In the science of government, Justice is policy. It is the only policy which God will tolerate. The nation which deserts it, and plunges into the labyrinth of Machiavelian diplomacy and double dealing, shall rue it. The science of government is the science of the distribution of Justice; equal and exact justice to all. Policy is a snare, and politicians, in the sense which that word has acquired in America, are a curse to us. What we want for our national prosperity, is simple, plain, straightforward Justice; so simple and so plain that a child can understand it. That is the justice of God as revealed in history, and revealed in the Scriptures of truth. That was the justice of the fathers and founders of this nation. Says Burke: "It is with the greatest difficulty that I attempt to separate policy from justice. Justice is itself the great standing policy of civil society, and any eminent departure from it, under any circumstances, lies under the suspicion of being no policy at all." Well may we give heed to these words of the great British statesman, for his was the most potent voice raised in the British parliament in behalf of American rights, at the period of the Revolution. Assuming this platform he breasted the whole fierce current of British prejudice and British policy. Policy said: We must have a revenue from America. Burke said: Be just. Justice is Policy. Hear the words of his speech on conciliation with America: "Slavery they can have anywhere. It is a weed that grows in every soil. They may have it from Spain; they may have it from Prussia; but, until you become lost to all feeling of your true interest and your natural dignity, freedom they can have only from you. * * Deny them this participation of freedom, and you break the sole bond which originally made, and must still preserve the unity of the empire. * * Do not entertain so weak an imagination as that your registers and your bonds, your affidavits and your sufferances, your cockets and your clearances, are what form the securities of your commerce. They are dead instruments, passive tools. It is the spirit of the English Constitution, which, infused through the mighty mass, pervades, feeds, unites, invigorates and vivifies every part of the empire, even down to the minutest member." Do you ask me what is the spirit of the English Constitution? It is Justice. That was Burke's policy as statesman. That was the pole-star of his political career. He fixed his eye upon it. No clouds of policy, or prejudice, or sophistry; no ridicule, or invective, or taunt, could dim his clear and perpetual vision of it. He believed in God. He believed that Justice is the key which unlocks the secrets of the government of God. He believed that God interposes in the processes and acts of human governments, and that he interposes always and only in the direction of the principles of divine and eternal justice. That faith raised him as a statesman and politician into sympathy and companionship with God. It made him a prophet.

My friends, let us not lose the benefit of the wisdom of our great transatlantic defender and friend. That whole wisdom had long before been summed up in the words of the inspired king of Israel: "The God of Israel said, the Rock of Israel spake to me, He that ruleth over men must be just, ruling in the fear of God." God was his teacher. Let him be ours. But what relevancy has this talk about justice to our present circumstances? Are we conscious of any wrong inflicted by our government upon the misguided men who have dared to lay their sacrilegious hands upon the ark of our liberties? Have we been guilty of any governmental act of injustice toward them? Let him who supposes so read the great speech of Alexander H. Stephens, made before the poisoned cup of secession had been forced to his lips, by a power as irresistible as that which forced the hemlock upon Socrates. Read his clear and brave words, asserting the great truth that the influence of the South had always controlled this Government. Read his distinct declaration of the wickedness of the doctrines of secession, and his prophetic description of its inevitable consequences. Those were the words of the Southern Vice-President sober, and none the less true that he has become intoxicated since, by a draught which he was compelled against his will to swallow. No, my friends, we have been guilty of no injustice to the South. What then was the cause of this war? Who was the author of it? God. "Whom God will destroy he first deprives of reason." Because we have been guilty of no injustice to the South, do you imagine that we stand as a nation *rectus in curia* before the bar of divine and eternal justice? What then does our President mean in asking us to implore the Divine Majesty to lead the whole nation through the paths of repentance back to the perfect enjoyment of union and fraternal peace? Whence come the throes of that moral volcano, whose fiery eruptions have darkened the whole heavens, and whose throbs of mortal agony seem to be rending the very earth beneath our feet, threatening to engulf the entire nation in one vast abyss and cataclysm of anarchy? You have witnessed the beginning of these eruptions even in the North. Last month you stood aghast with horror before the savage outburst of the elements of social depravity and crime in a neighboring city. To-day you are fearing it in your own. You owe your opportunity of meeting in God's house to-day,* you owe your immunity from sack and pillage, from the incendiary's torch and the assassin's knife, to no fear of God, to no restraints of civil law, to no arguments addressed to the reason and conscience of men, but simply to a wholesome respect for grape-shot and bayonets. What is the true significance of these awful and portentous moral phenomena? There can be but one true answer. There is a God, and Justice is his name. As a nation we have been arraigned before the throne of the all-Just, and we have been found guilty. "The principles and elements upon which regular gravitations in the moral order depend, have begun to murmur." Begun to murmur! They have been murmuring for years, and we refused to hear their monitory voice. "There have been mysterious moanings in the deeps, which the heavens have heard," though we heard them not. "Reeking blood," lacerated backs, muscles torn by blood-hounds, and scarred by bullets, violated and corrupted chastity, sundered families, "weeping mothers," humanity plundered of every right which the Decalogue secures—"these have been formidable pleaders" against us. Cotton has proclaimed himself King, not of earth merely, but of heaven also. He has made a new Decalogue, a new Christianity, a new Bible. He hath opposed and exalted himself above all that is called God, or that is worshiped; so that he, as God, hath seated himself in the temple of God, showing himself that he

* During the Draft in Buffalo.

is God. And as a nation we have been worshiping at the shrine of this Baal. That worship has corrupted us. It has corrupted our politics, corrupted our national legislature, corrupted our state legislatures, corrupted our elections, corrupted our judiciary, corrupted and choked all the channels of executive justice, corrupted our very Christianity, rendering it necessary for the ministers of Christ to preach the Ten Words of Jehovah and the Eight Words of Jesus with a timid and faltering voice, with a qualifying *but*, and an exceptive *if*. "It is time that this vast" power which has thrown its huge bulk square athwart the current of an incorrupt Christianity, yea, athwart the currents of the world's civilization and humanity, "should fall." These convulsions are the voice of God. They proclaim, as with the blast of the archangel's trumpet, that "the moment has come for Incorruptible Supreme Equity to look to it." King Cotton "has been impeached before the Infinite, and his fall is decreed." This blasphemous Power "has vexed God." What remains? It remains that as a people we put ourselves in sympathy with the Executive Justice of the Almighty, or that we fall before the mandates of its Power. The day of reasoning and rebuke and expostulation has gone by; and the day of retribution has come. The throes of the great earthquake which is to sink this Babylon of iniquity are "shaking the nations." The day of God's vengeance has come. It is the year of recompenses for the controversy of Zion. The streams have been turned into pitch, and the dust into brimstone. God is treading the wine-press alone, and of the people there has been none with him. He is treading us in his anger. He is trampling us in his fury. Our blood is sprinkling his garments. It hath stained all his raiment. For the day of vengeance is in his heart, and the year of his redeemed is come.

III.—*A third condition of success in this struggle is, that we put ourselves under the guidance of the Wisdom of God.*

We have been under the guidance of that human folly which dignifies itself with the name of statesmanship, long enough. It has plunged the nation into a civil war whose vast proportions will be the great landmark of the nineteenth century, down to the close of human history. What the government needs is the wisdom which cometh from God. The interest which our rulers ask, in our supplications to-day, is, that we invoke God's Holy Spirit, "to guide the counsels of the government with wisdom adequate to so great a national emergency." Never did men more imperatively need it. For never did a body of rulers stand in more exigent circumstances, or under more fearful responsibilities to liberty and civilization; to humanity and to God. Never were rulers placed in a position more novel, and never were any called to walk a path more feebly illuminated by the light of political precedents, or by the maxims of political prudence. Is it any wonder that they have made mistakes? The true wonder is, that they have not made shipwreck of the Republic. A pilot with a keener vision than theirs has had his eye upon the binnacle; a pilot with a sturdier strength has had his hand upon the helm of the ship of State. The Wisdom of God has been over the government, vouchsafed in answer to the penitent prayers of his people. It is a wisdom which converts human weakness into strength, and human blunders into the highest skill; a wisdom which makes even

> "our indiscretions serve us well,
> When our deep plots do fail."

He who can read the history of this contest, and not see the Wisdom of God in it, must be wilfully and, therefore, hopelessly blind. Look at the condition of the nation at the opening of the war: its treasury empty, its arsenals plundered and stripped by traitors; its little army and navy scattered by an administration servilely subservient to treason, the one to the ends of the land, the other to the ends of the earth; its enemies confident, arrogant, boastful, insulting, threatening instantly to plant their felon flag upon the dome of the capitol, and to entertain their bastard government in the halls of the White House. Look at the condition of the nation now: its treasury well supplied, its credit so high that the people are pouring their loans at this moment into its coffers at the rate of a million a day; its arsenals stored with all the munitions of war; its army of citizen soldiers swarming in every part of the land, their bugles singing peans of victory whose strains awaken the echoes of the mountains and float away over the sea; its navy, created as if by magic, threading every river, watching every port — an arm of war which has already rendered obsolete all the ancient fortresses of Christendom, and whose rapidly increasing strength gives promise that the nation which wields it in the cause of justice and civilization will soon be able to sweep the ocean, and to stand against the world in arms. Its enemies; look at *them:* cowed, starved, humiliated, and the insolent brag of chivalry taken out of them forever. Are these the works of a weak, stupid, foolish, God-forsaken government? No, they are the works of a government which has sought, and in some measure at least received, from God a wisdom which is above their own. They acknowledge it, and they earnestly ask us to invoke the Divine Majesty to guide their counsels in the future. What then, as touching the Divine wisdom, remains for us to do? Two things. First, pray for our rulers. Secondly, obey them. First, Pray for them. Our own interest demands it. Their cause is our cause. If God's wisdom does not guide them, our cause is ruined. They actually man the ship of State. They cannot be got out of it until the constitutional period arrives. If God's wisdom does not guide them they will steer wild, and the vessel which bears the whole precious heritage of our liberties will go head on upon the breakers. The word of God demands it. "I exhort, therefore, that first of all, supplications, prayers, intercessions and giving of thanks be made for all men: For kings and for all that are in authority, that we may lead a quiet and peaceable life, in all godliness and honesty." Secondly, Obey them. The word of God demands this also. "Let every soul be subject to the higher powers. For there is no power but of God. The powers that be are ordained of God. Whosoever, therefore, resisteth the power resisteth the ordinance of God, and they shall receive to themselves damnation." Our own interest demands it. If our free government, if the great American Magna Charta are to be saved at all, they are to be saved by the prompt, decided, and efficient efforts of our rulers, guided in their action by the wisdom of Almighty God, and cordially and loyally supported by the people. All popular insubordination, all factious opposition to the measures of the government, all dragging down of the great issues upon which our national life depend, into the dirty arena of party politics, into the contemptible squabble for place and power, is a crime against liberty and a crime against God. But what then; are we to permit those, who for the moment happen to have the custody of the precious heritage bequeathed us by our fathers, to destroy it? Are we to permit the great sun of American Freedom to be plucked from the heavens by the hand of a tyrant? Are we to permit its blessed beams to be put out, by arbitrary arrests, by the suspension of the writ of habeas corpus; by exiling the citizens of the country for exercising their natural liberty of speech; by forcing poor day-laborers into the ranks of the army, and permitting the rich to go free? Are not these things going to blot out forever the great and glorious sun of American liberty? My friends, I have read of an astronomer, a profound student and worshiper of the *sun*, who once beheld a fearful phenomenon, which threatened utterly to annihilate the great luminary of the world. Intent upon his observations touching the luminous atmosphere of the sun, he suddenly beheld a spectacle which chilled his soul with horror. A huge, black monster, of gigantic proportions, mounted one edge of its disc, spread his vast bulk along its surface, obscured its blessed beams, and slowly marched forward, apparently devouring as he went; a living, moving, visible, incontestable demonstration of the Hindu theory of eclipses. The philosopher's heart ceased to beat. His blood froze in his veins. What was to become of our poor world when the sun should be devoured? What was to become of the vegetable and animate tribes of earth, wrapped in the Cimmerian blackness of an endless night? Poor astronomer! Thou art needlessly alarmed. It is only a fly crossing the upper lens of thy telescope.

*But the war has been perverted from its original and legitimate design. Its design was to save the Union. It has been converted into a war for freeing the negro.* I deny the truth of the proposition. I shall not deny that *God's* object in this war may be to wipe out forever from this continent the Institution of Negro Slavery. I solemnly believe that it is. But that is not now, and never has been, the object of the government. The whole history of the discussion of this subject brands such an assertion as false to facts, as well as false to the express declaration of the President himself. Politic or impolitic, no honest man has any right to deny that the emancipation proclamation and the arming of the negro were measures adopted avowedly as a military necessity for conquering a peace and restoring the integrity of the Union.

*But it was impolitic. The negro can never be made to fight; an army of negroes, at the first cannon shot, will flee in confusion like a flock of sheep.* Let the Floridian campaign, let Milliken's Bend and Port Hudson and Fort Wagner answer that libel upon the negro character, and prove him to be a fighter even if he is not allowed to be a man.

*But it was impolitic, nevertheless; for white troops can never be made to fight, side by side, with black ones.* False again to facts. Doubtless some of our troops shared in the common prejudices of the country against the negro. But they have learned already to respect his martial qualities, and are only too glad to substitute the effusion of a portion of black blood for a portion of their own, in conquering a peace which the troops engaged in the actual tug of war in the Cotton States are entirely convinced never can be conquered whilst four millions of black hands are employed in building the forts which they are to storm, and in feeding the men whose batteries and bayonets they are to breast in the work of restoring the Union.

*But arming the negro is impolitic still. It exasperates the South, and renders hopeless all efforts for conciliation.* My friends, this is not a question of conciliating the rebels of the South. It is a question of conquering them. Who talks of conciliating rebels with arms in their hands, scornfully and persistently repudiating every idea of a reconstruction of the Union, and marking their career of crime by a violation of all the laws of civilized warfare? Men may "Cry

Peace, Peace. But there is no Peace." It is war, and only war, till the flag of the Union floats on every fortress from Canada to the Gulf.

*But the nation will be financially ruined. It will be loaded with a burden of debt which will grind it to powder.* What then are we to do? Give up? Go back? That is to slump into the abyss of anarchy. It is national repudiation. It is universal bankruptcy. The more vigorous and effective the war the shorter it will be. The shorter it is the less the national debt. Brought to a close, as speedily as a united and truly loyal people have it perfectly in their power to bring it to a close, the national debt will be nothing to us. It will be like the fly in the fable settled upon the horn of the ox. Doubtless the government has made mistakes. Doubtless it will continue to make them. But I firmly believe its aim to be loyal, and its main policy to have been guided by the wisdom of God. Let him who doubts it divide the war into two great periods: the period antedating the emancipation proclamation, and the period succeeding it. Let him count the disasters and the victories; let him measure their magnitude and importance, in each period, and rest satisfied that God is with us and that his hand has guided us.

*But suppose we conquer, what is to be done with the negro?* My friends, that is not a question for to-day. Let us not climb the mountain before we reach it. Sufficient for the day is the evil thereof. If God gives our rulers wisdom to conduct the war to a successful issue, let us have faith to believe that he will give them wisdom equal to the solution of any ulterior question of policy or duty which may arise.

IV.—*It remains to say, in a word, in the fourth place, that a final condition of success in the war is, that we make ourselves instruments of the Mercy of God.*

God is wise, and God is just; but he is merciful also. Merciful, not to haughty rebels who insult his authority, and hurl down the gauntlet of defiance at his feet; but to the humble and the afflicted, to the poor and the oppressed. His heart of infinite compassion has had quite as much to do with the origin and conduct of this war as the attribute of his Justice which it is so gloriously signalizing. God has solemnly declared that all souls are his. He loves the black man as well the white. Christ died as truly for him as for the white man. He feels as tenderly for his sorrows and he will as certainly and as signally avenge his wrongs. The prejudice against the black man in America is as vulgar as it is wicked. It exists nowhere in Christendom but here. What Christian is willing any longer to harbor in his bosom a sentiment whose brutal outbreak in New York has revealed its true character, has stripped it of every attribute, I do not say that ennobles humanity, but that makes it respectable; that discriminates a man from a brute! But the Providence of God does not seem to call us at present to interfere in any special manner in behalf of the black man, except it be to protect him from violence. God has assumed himself the advocacy of his cause, and I am willing to trust it there. But there are other directions, in which he calls upon us, through all the tender voices of patriotism, of parental, fraternal and sisterly affection, to make ourselves the instruments of his divine compassion. Who won the glorious victories for which a nation brings its oblation of praise into God's temples to-day? Our fathers and our sons; our husbands and our brothers. As we stand worshiping here where are they? Toiling, multitudes of them, beneath the fervors of a Southern sun. Sleeping peacefully, multitudes of them — peacefully, though in bloody shrouds, that dreamless sleep which knows no waking. Drop a tear, in the midst of your thanksgiving, over the new-heaped mounds scattered thick through all the land, from Maine to Florida, from Texas to the sea, which tell so many aching hearts that fathers and sons, that husbands and brothers, are hidden forever from their eyes; — gone forever beyond the embraces of their love. They rest in God. Leave them upon the bosom of his infinite love; and turn your eyes to the vast hospitals which this "cruel rebellion" has filled to repletion with our wounded, sick and dying defenders. Is it possible for us, amid our songs of thanksgiving, to forget them to-day? How are we to remember them? In what spirit are we to comply with the President's proclamation, and ask God "to visit with tender care and consolation, throughout the length and breadth of our land, all those who through the vicissitudes of marches, voyages, battles and sieges, have been brought to suffer in mind, body and estate"? We are to make ourselves the ministers of the mercy which we supplicate, the almoners of the infinite compassions of the heart of our God. And what additional cause of thanksgiving have we to-day that the good Providence of God has furnished us not only with the pecuniary means but with open channels for these ministrations of mercy. Unable to go in persons to our mutilated and suffering friends, who have sacrificed every thing for our protection, let us thank God for the labors of the Sanitary Commission; let us thank him especially for the noble regiment of good Samaritans, now one thousand strong, whose unpaid labors are guided and sustained by the United States Christian Commission. Upon what recent battle-field have not these messengers of mercy been found? what hospital has remained unvisited by the ministrations of their love? At Shiloh, in the peninsular campaign, in the battles before Washington, in the Maryland invasion, at Fredericksburg, in the Pennsylvania invasion, at Camp Convalescent, Camp Parole, Point Lookout, through the long line of the Mississippi, everywhere where the sick and wounded and dying soldier was to be found, there have these angels of mercy sped their way, bearing in one hand medicaments for the body, and in the other the balm of Gilead for the sick and wounded soul. O how often has the eye of the dying soldier, prostrate and alone upon the battle-field, when the storm of war had swept over his mutilated body and its roar had died away in the distance, beamed with joy at the sight of the silver badge of the Christian Commission! How often, his parching thirst assuaged, his wounds bound up and comforted, has that eye been raised to the cross of Jesus and beheld the Lamb of God who taketh away the sins of the world! How often has his last prayer been breathed to God for his blessing upon the Christian Commission! I cannot descend into particulars. It is not necessary. You know this Commission. The ladies of Buffalo, especially, have sympathized most zealously and effectively in its labor of love. You know its works. And you will not fail to make it the channel of your liberal thank-offerings to-day.

One word more and I have done. I have endeavored to set before you, conscientiously and fearlessly, my deep and abiding convictions touching the religious conditions of our further success in the terrible war which afflicts this nation. I may have been mistaken in the application of these truths. I am sure I am not mistaken in the truths themselves. We must acknowledge the hand of God in this war; we must put ourselves in sympathy with the Justice of God; we must seek the guidance of the Wisdom of God; we must make ourselves the ministers of Mercy of God. Fulfilling these conditions we may confidently claim the fulfillment of the promise of the text, for that promise rests upon eternal principles. "The Lord shall cause thine enemies that rise up against thee to be smitten before thy face; they shall come out against thee one way, and shall flee before thee seven ways." Fulfilling these conditions, this war will reach a speedy and glorious conclusion. Come that glad day! May our eyes be permitted to behold it, for its blessed light will shine upon a free Bible, a free pulpit, a free nation, inhabited everywhere and only by free men, lifting up unfettered hands to the God and Father of every human soul. Then will we celebrate another day of National Thanksgiving. Then our song shall be the song of Moses and the Lamb: "Great and marvellous are thy works, Lord God Almighty: just and true are thy ways, thou King of Saints: Who shall not fear thee, O Lord, and glorify thy name, for thou only art holy; for all nations shall come and worship before thee, for thy judgments are made manifest."

www.ingramcontent.com/pod-product-compliance
Lightning Source LLC
LaVergne TN
LVHW011132110826
845150LV00008B/2301

* 9 7 8 1 4 1 8 1 9 3 9 7 3 *